T0142524

SELF LOVE ....
LOVESELF.....

BRÉCHA BYRD

authorHOUSE®

AuthorHouse™
1663 Liberty Drive
Bloomington, IN 47403
www.authorhouse.com
Phone: 1 (800) 839-8640

Published by AuthorHouse 11/25/2019

ISBN: 978-1-7283-2465-4 (sc)
ISBN: 978-1-7283-2464-7 (e)

Library of Congress Control Number: 2019912653

Print information available on the last page.

This book is printed on acid-free paper.

for girls all over the world … there is

absolutely *nothing* wrong with you

you are *not* the problem . . . you are the *solution*

Self Love...L O V E S E L F

period.

"You're so **u g l y**."

"You smile **t o o** much."

"You're too **d a r k**."

"You're **m e a n** and **b o s s y**."

"You're too **s t r o n g**."

"You look like a **m a n**."

Those were just some of the things other girls said to me in school. Yet, ever since I was a little girl, my mother and father told me that I was beautiful. They said that I have the most beautiful skin, the most concerned eyes, and the most unique legs. They told me that my heart was filled with love and care. My mother would always say that my eyebrows were beautifully made and my thighs were thick with confidence. She told me that my hair, with all of the fuzz, was gorgeous. She said that my wide nose was lovely. She told me that my height was not abnormal, but it was exceptional. For a very long time, I believed those words my mother and father said. They encouraged me. The words uplifted me. Throughout school, I treated people with respect. I cared for people of all circumstances. I believed in them. It was not until fifth grade when all of those words began to fade. Suddenly, my "beautiful skin" was "too dark and ugly". My "concerned eyes" were "too slanted and bare". My "unique legs" were "too long". My heart was filled with echoes of the words of my enemies' "manipulation and jealousy". My eyebrows were compared to a two year old's artwork. My thighs were "too fat" and my nose was "too big". My fuzzy hair was "nappy and unattractive" and my height was compared to a man. Some girls in my grade hated almost everything about me. I never really understood why. I was not invited to some parties, was criticized for my appearance daily, and was excluded from conversations with certain people. I was bullied because I was being myself. Some girls in my grade H A T E D that I was the person that I was. For the longest time, I thought that I was the problem. I thought I was the issue. I thought everything about me was an accident made by God. I thought that I was not beautiful. I thought everything those girls said was true. People betrayed me, hated me, and avoided me. I was depressed. I felt as if I had committed a crime and was sentenced to prison. My eating decreased because I desired to be skinny, I wore long sleeve shirts, even if it was warm, to hide my ugly skin, and I tried not to show my hips by wearing baggy clothing. I thought that hiding the real me would allow me to fit their standards of "beautiful". I was young, gullible, and imperfect. I began to realize that there was nothing I could do to fit their standards. Throughout this whole phase, my family stuck by my side. My parents encouraged me to look myself in the mirror everyday and say, "I AM BEAUTIFUL". I would look at my Asian eyes and my protruding lips, and find beauty within. I would look at my long legs and be amazed at how much I had grown. I examined my dark skin and found it so defined and rich with color. I was beginning to love myself once again. My parents preached principles that helped me regain self-love.

1. TRUST G O D

The road to loving yourself is a journey. According to Google, a journey is an act of traveling from one place to another. From my perspective, a journey is an act of traveling, changing, or rerouting from one place to another or one's outlook or perspective. Basically, our lives are journeys. We have different paths, fates, and destinies. The journey is how we get there. **In order to love yourself, you must love God. He places people in our lives to teach us. Everything, good or bad, happens for a reason. It can be a lesson and a blessing. It is all a part of His plan.** God's son, Jesus, died on the cross for us so we would not perish. God's mercy endures forever. That's love, PERIODT. God's love is something we cannot take for granted. Jesus paid the price and God's love is freely given to us. One cannot truly love oneself without loving God. He is the beginning and the end. He is an awesome God. Obstacles will be thrown in your direction, but with Him, you can overcome.

My great grandmother used to sing me this song with these lyrics, "No weapon formed against me, shall prosper." My cousin named Journey and her friend Aiesha were the ultimate best friend goals, until one evening Journey beat Aiesha in a talent show. Journey and

Aiesha were no longer best friends anymore. It seemed that Aiesha was angry with Journey because Journey won. Aiesha stopped talking to Journey and acted as if she was invisible. It made me so sad to see Journey empty. For awhile, Journey was stressed and confused. Never in her life would she have thought that this was going to happen. Journey yearned for a friend, a true friend, someone who was almost as good a friend as Aiesha. Journey thought their friendship meant more than a stupid contest, but unfortunately, that was not so. Journey constantly tried to reconcile with Aiesha but it never worked out. All of the slumber parties, trips, and fun days together were over. Little did Journey know that she would learn from all of this. Journey began to trust God. She grew up in the church and heard testimonies of trusting God but had never really done it herself. She had to know her worth, be herself, shine her light, regardless of how Aiesha was, and trust God. That is exactly what she did. All of your friends that you have today will not always be there for you. Some will come and some will go. It is all a part of God's plan, He knows. You learn from the people around you.

A couple of years later, Journey became friends with three interesting guys. Kyle, Isaac, and Jeremiah. They were the new and improved "clique". People questioned Journey as to why she kept hanging out with the guys. Truth was, she needed friends and they were there. They listened to Journey and connected with her in a beautiful way. They made her laugh and never showed negativity towards her. They were angels in their own unique way. Although Kyle and Journey fell off, Isaac and Jeremiah remained loyal, all a part of God's plan, indeed.

2. Knowing Your W O R T H

Now, what does that mean exactly? From my perspective, knowing your worth means not settling for anything mediocre. In life, people will try to belittle you if you pose as a threat to them. Rachel, a girl at my school, consistently tried to devalue me. She wanted me to feel like I was an outsider. She wanted me to feel alone and worthless. Honestly, sometimes I did. Girls can be so mean at times. I began to talk with my family about the issue and they encouraged me to be who I was. I believed that I was more valuable than what Rachel said. I believed that I knew who I was and would continue to be that person. **Knowing your worth means that you are aware and accept your value. You are a precious jewel. We all are. When we try to actually realize our worth, we may become discouraged.** On the lines below, write why/how you know your worth.

I know my W O R T H because.......

_____

_____

_____

Whether you realize it or not, simply writing those words can carry you a long way. Knowing your worth will allow you to grow. **You write your own story, so let your growth speak for itself. Speak in silence. EVOLVE so you can RESOLVE.** Believe those words. If you do this, you are one step closer to loving yourself.

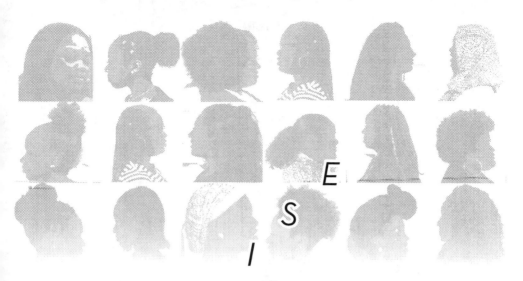

3. R **Above**

Okay, here we go. On March 19, 2018, I turned 16! The morning of my birthday was so beautiful. It was not too hot, not too cold; it was just right. I wore a beautiful yellow dress and my cousin took pictures of me that morning before I left for school. Arriving at school, people crowded me with love and happiness while saying, "Happy Birthday, Lola!" In fact, one of my favorite people, named Twists, made me a jumbo card! The card was awesome and tears of joy filled my eyes. The day before my birthday, I told my sista Liz that I was getting my hair done. She was excited. I was too. However, my classmate Vanessa was not. She asked me abruptly, "What are you getting done to your hair??"

I responded with, "You will see tomorrow."

Fast forward to twenty four hours later, and my hair was soft as a pillow with luscious curls and rich with ethnicity. My hair was beautiful. The bell rang and everyone dispersed into their first block. Coincidentally, Vanessa was in my first block. Unbothered, I examined my phone to text my Grams to say thank you when I heard Vanessa call my name.

"Lola!" she said in a hateful voice.

I remained examining my phone.

"Lola. So, that's what you got done to your HAIR???" she said disgustingly.

Immediately, inappropriate words aimed at her filled my brain. I turned around and looked at her. I smiled.

She then said, "Cause I thought you were going to get something better like braids or something."

I smiled at her continuously and turned back around in my seat. I told myself that she is jealous and that I don't even need to entertain her bullsh*t, excuse my language young people, but it was the truth. I thought to myself, God woke me up this morning on my sixteenth birthday to live to inspire, breathe, be thankful, show love, and to have a blessed day. God didn't want me to fuss or become upset because of envious people. I had to walk away, I had to realize my worth, and I had to RISE ABOVE the ignorance and negativity. I am a child of God, okay? I will not let one of Satan's followers knock me off my path to greatness. **Sometimes in life, people will try to make you feel worthless, even on your birthday. You have to RISE ABOVE!** Vanessa wanted me to get out of my character, cuss her out, and have a bad day. But I thought no! No weapon formed against me shall prosper. **My confidence, my worth, and my faith are more important and valuable than any negative comment that a hater says. I love me, I know me, and I rise above the negativity. PERIODT.**

4. Believing I N Y O U

When you believe in yourself, then you can be yourself. **To believe in yourself does not only take strength, it takes acceptance. To believe in every flaw, imperfection, and unique trait about you is so important. Yes, we all have flaws, imperfections, and unique traits but you do not have to be ashamed of them, you E M B R A C E them.** So many negative people also known as haters have tried to discourage every different thing about me. My height and eyebrows were the top two targets. I remember when I was at a summer camp and a counselor consistently questioned me about my eyebrows around numerous kids. She asked, "So, do you use an eyebrow pencil everyday?" I often ignored such questions, but everyone was staring so I had to answer.

I responded with, "Yes, I do."

She added, "Why?? That's weird." Everyone laughed.

I wanted to burst into tears. I literally wanted to get my phone, cry to my parents, and beg them to come and get me. I have extremely thin eyebrows and to the world, that was weird. Even today, I still struggle with the whole makeup thing everyday, but at that camp, I had to be strong. I later told my parents about this incident and they were furious that the so called "counselor" belittled me. My father told me that I was beautiful. He said that I was beautiful inside and out. He told me to always be who I am and to believe in myself. From that day, I did what my father said. I began to believe in myself. I began to believe in my eyebrows and that they were beautiful with or without makeup. At school it was still a struggle. Girls and guys laughed at my eyebrows and picked on me. It is going to be difficult loving your flaws and imperfections, but it is possible. **Surround yourself with positive people. Lift each other up. Empower each other. When we stand together, as one, there is nobody that can stop us, not one.**

5. SHINING YOUR LIGHT

Once you know your worth and believe in yourself then you can shine your L I G H T. On the lines below, write what you think "SHINE YOUR LIGHT" means.

I think "SHINE YOUR LIGHT" means

_____

_____

_____

_____

We all have gifts. Whether it be playing the piano like Alicia, singing like Beyoncé, dunking like LeBron, kicking like Messi, dancing like Chris Brown or writing poetry like my sis JaLea Moody, we all have gifts that need to shine and be shared throughout the world. Shining your light inspires people to not be afraid to be great. People are sometimes scared that others will criticize or devalue their gifts. If one girl shines her light, it is very difficult for others to dim. My friend Becky is a really great soccer player and so was I. We both would shine our lights together and that made us better. But unfortunately, there were some who envied our success. On multiple occasions, some of our teammates did not pass us the ball during the games. At first, we brushed it off, but eventually, our coaches, fans, and parents noticed what was going on. There was a meeting held about the recurring issues on our team and eventually, it began to diminish. That was a learning lesson for Becky and me. It is amazing how you think everyone is rooting for you, but in reality, there are some who are not reppin' for you (FACTS!!). To be honest, that should fuel you to want to shine your light even more. What do you have to lose? The answer is nothing.

When I was 13, I participated in a gala where the winner would be crowned princess based on the content in her essay about the importance of fathers. My father has been in my life ever since I was born so I did not really grasp how it felt to be fatherless. Some of my classmates' fathers were not present in their lives and I saw some of the effects this had on them. I decided to write everything I saw. My essay was awesome, I received the throne and a standing ovation! My father was so proud. **One of the sponsors of the event told me this, "Miss Lola Lakes, the light that is in you cannot be touched." His words spoke life into me. S H I N E Y O U R L I G H T!!! And as my mother always says, "Don't dim it for anybody."**

Each of you can inspire anyone, no matter the age. You are never too young to make change.

6. NEVER L O S E YOURSELF IN SOMEONE E L S E

While partaking on this beautiful journey of self love, it is very important to put you first. Your feelings, your thoughts, and your emotions must come first. You cannot continue to please everyone around you without securing yourself initially because no matter how hard you try, it still won't be enough. I witnessed this first hand. I was involved with a guy who was never satisfied with me. Regardless of my unconditional love, extraordinary support, and enhanced effort towards him, he still did me dirty. I gave him so many chances. There were numerous red flags that I disregarded because he told me he changed but in actuality, he didn't. I saw potential in him and fell in love with it. **LADIES, DO NOT FALL IN LOVE WITH POTENTIAL! FALL IN LOVE WITH YOURSELF!** Trust me, no matter how many times you bring him to church, or how many beautiful flowers he brings when he messes up, **YOU CANNOT CHANGE OR FIX HIM. I repeat YOU CANNOT CHANGE OR FIX HIM.** The only way he will change is if he allows God to change him. The only person you can control is yourself. You allow his actions towards you. You allow whether or not he gets what he wants from you, whenever he wants it. Once again, you have to KNOW YOUR WORTH especially in times like this.

If you truly love yourself, do not keep allowing him to hurt you over and over again. When is the line going to be drawn? Listen, I know it's hard. When you've created a bond with someone, the two of you become almost inseparable, and as time passes by, things reveal themselves and you have to make a very difficult decision, that process is very frustrating. You will miss the good times and desire to have them back but you have to be strong! Remember how he made you feel when he hurt you over and over again and all of the pain he caused when all you did was LOVE HIM. You loved him and that was hurting you. You loved him and he could not handle it. You loved him and he did not appreciate it. **When it came to relationships or situationships, I knew that being with me was an opportunity, privilege, and blessing all in one. How did I know? I knew my worth. I knew what I brought to the table. I am not for everyone. My body is not for everyone. My heart cannot be given to everyone because some people are not worthy of it.** Yes, you will think you miss him but in actuality, the person you think you miss, really did not even exist. **If at first he was an attraction, then became a distraction, you need to perform subtraction.**

7. LEARN + ABOUT = YOU

This practice is very difficult for some people. **To love yourself, you have to know yourself. You have to set your standards and understand you.** So many people are lost and do not know who they are. Spend time with just you, listen to the things you say, and learn about you. Notice how you respond to different situations. Focus on you.

There was a girl at my school named Anne. Anne was very energetic but easily influenced. Anne did not have a mind of her own. She would let girls use her just so she could be their "friend". I am sure there is an Anne at every school, the girl that tries to fit in but never does, the girl that gets bullied because of her stunning curls or the girl that almost killed herself because everyone picked on her. Anne never knew who she truly was because she always tried to be someone else. Anne began to learn about herself and instantly fell in love with the real her. Anne was no longer Anne because of her self love. She became AnnaMarie. AnnaMarie was who she was always meant to be. AnnaMarie was inside her the entire time. Anne just had to love her kind. AnnaMarie was her birth name, a name she truly loved, yet everyone else called her Anne because AnnaMarie was not "cool" enough. **No matter what, always stay true to yourself. Never let your pride, insecurities, and flaws determine who you are. Once again, embrace every unique thing about you.** Do not use them to disguise the real you. THE REAL YOU - embraces who you are, acts how you feel, and enjoys what you do.

Some people have so much ego and pride that they are unwilling to accept the truth. That is why confidence is a necessity to loving yourself. Stay true, be you, and always keep it real. So many people are unhappy with what they possess or their circumstances. So many people desire to have more instead of being grateful for what they already have. So many people do not realize what they have until it is gone. This is because of lack of contentment. Being happy is so important when traveling Route Self-Love. **You have to be content with who you are in order to love you.** Embrace the real you because you are one in a million. **Do not let someone's negative spirit alter your positive spirit. People will try to decrease your positivity to increase theirs. You have to rise above and not stoop down to their level. Be the bigger person and be happy!**

8.BE KIND & HEAL YOUR MIND

Without the love of Christ and loving yourself, one cannot show genuine love to others. This is where kindness steps in. Simply being nice to someone can brighten his/her day. **You never know what a person is going through. Years from now, how you looked or how popular you were will not matter. What will matter is how you treated people**. Treat people with respect. Be happy for people. Jealousy is so unattractive, yet so many people possess it. People feel envy because they do not have what another person has so they blame the other person for it. Confusing, right?

I was faced with Jealousy throughout school. She had short hair and deceitful eyes. Anyway, Jealousy envied me. She envied everything positive about me. My strong personality, my unstoppable will, and my multiple wits were a threat to her. Numerous times, I tried to be her friend, but she did not want us to become friends. She would talk about me behind my back to my closest friends; she tried to belittle my large and awesome afro, and lastly, she had the nerve to act like I was below her even though my name was always in her mouth. It was a tough time for me honestly, and if I were not emotionally strong, there is no telling what could have happened to me. There was a time when I tried out for a dance team and three girls talked "junk" the entire auditions. They made comments like, "She is too tall to be a dancer. She is too strong and built to be a dancer. She has a penis. She should play football." Thank God that I brushed those haters off like some dirt but what if I didn't? What if I didn't? What if I let what they said eat my confidence day by day, piece by piece, bit by bit? Maybe I would be in a mental hospital. Maybe I would not be writing this book. Maybe this book would have never existed.

It is so important to heal your mind. Your mind is your power and it controls everything. It controls the way you think, feel, and ultimately, how you act. It is so important for your mind to have peace and constantly be filled with outpourings of positivity! If you need to eat ice cream, pray, listen to soothing music, or drink hot tea to relax your mind, then by all means, do what you have to do. I'm telling you, if your mind has peace, a burden will be lifted off of you emotionally, mentally, spiritually, and physically. You do not have to forget, but you have to forgive people, and you have to forgive yourself. **All of the mistakes you have made or bad decisions you have encountered do not determine your destiny. It is what you do after the adversity that matters. Will you give up and not try or get smarter and stronger to live your best life? BE KIND AND HEAL YOUR MIND!**

9. S. Y. W. P. P.

On the lines below, write down what you think **S. Y. W. P. P.** means.

S. _____

Y. _____

W. _____

P. _____

P. _____

I bet what you came up with is hilarious! Anyway, **S. Y. W. P. P.** means

....

SURROUND

YOURSELF

WITH

POSITIVE

PEOPLE

This is so important because like the saying goes, birds of a feather, flock together. It is so easy to criticize and judge folk when

you hang around the criticizable type. Around middle school through high school years, anyone who seems "different" is belittled. For what reason? Because you do not have the new Js? You are the tallest kid in the school? You are smarter than some of your teachers? You are too focused on your future that you do not have time for immaturity? Those things about you should not be simmered down, they should be embraced. They make you, you! This happens a lot on social media! Instagram, Snapchat, and Twitter are a few areas of entertainment for our generation and the generations to come. Now, I will admit that I do enjoy these apps. These social platforms should be used for positivity but often create drama, disputes, and peer pressure due to certain users. Young ladies of excellence, the truth is, if you use social media to compete with other people and compare yourself to them, it will drive you insane. You will constantly find yourself unhappy and easily influenced by anything or anyone just to "fit in". STAND OUT IN A POSITIVE WAY. Use social media to share what you have experienced and learned throughout the world and encourage or inspire others to spread love and light all while having fun. Social media should be fun but not because you are bullying or belittling someone. Some of us are afraid to stand out for this reason. If you surround yourself with positive people, you will embrace others and yourself. First, you have to ensure that you are a positive person. Looking at the glass half full, seeing the bright side of situations, and finding a solution instead of dwelling on the problem allow you to become a more positive person. **We all need to lift each other up. The world will become so much better when we do so. Do not compare and contrast yourself with others. It is okay to compliment each other.**

10. Be CONFIDENT
Not Cocky

When on the road to loving yourself, you absolutely need to know the difference between being **CONFIDENT** and being **cocky**. Let's play a game. Below are written scenarios and I need you to circle either **CONFIDENT** or **cocky**.

1. I am me. I am beautiful and unique.

    Circle.

    CONFIDENT   **cocky**

2. I am the prettiest girl in the world and everybody else is below me.

    Circle.

    CONFIDENT   **cocky**

3. Nobody has what I have because I am better than them.

    Circle.

    CONFIDENT   **cocky**

4. I can do all things through Christ who strengthens me.

Circle.

CONFIDENT cocky

5. I am the best. Everything I do, I do it right.

Circle.

CONFIDENT cocky

6. I believe that I can accomplish anything if I put my mind to it.

Circle.

CONFIDENT cocky

7. I don't need anybody because I'm proof of perfection.

Circle.

CONFIDENT cocky

8. Every girl wishes she was me.

Circle.

CONFIDENT cocky

There are no right or wrong answers to this game but it is a great exercise to see where you stand exactly. The answers that I circled were the following:

1. **CONFIDENT**

2. **cocky**

3. **cocky**

4. **CONFIDENT**

5. ~~**cocky**~~

6. **CONFIDENT**

7. **cocky**

8. **cocky**

Personally, when one empowers herself and speaks positively about herself without bringing anyone else down, that shows confidence. When one speaks boastfully of herself or himself and puts someone down, that shows cockiness. It is so important to understand the difference between the two. You will be mistaken for someone you are not if you accidentally display cockiness when attempting to be confident. I can honestly say to be confident is not an easy task. In life, you have constant arrows being thrown at you for attempting and desiring to be confident. **When you are confident, you do not only show it, you own it. It is like another accessory. You wear it, and no matter what, you rock it.** There will be some who admire your confidence. There will be some who yearn for your confidence. There will be some who envy your confidence. And yes, there will be some who are threatened by your confidence. Crazy, right? **How can someone be threatened by you because you are**

attempting to better and be yourself? I had a very difficult time trying to answer this question. Even today, I am still puzzled as to why someone who could not care less if I died is the same person who worried about me trying to grow in every way. I wish everyone could be happy for everyone, but it does not work like that. People are often threatened by someone because they possess something the other person does not have.

11. LOVE THE SKIN YOU'RE IN.... IT COMES FROM WITHIN

To love yourself, you must love the skin you're in. To complete this task, it comes from within! You have to believe the complexion of your skin is beautiful. I am a darker sista. My melanin is evident and there were many times people have said to me "Lola, you're pretty for a dark skin girl." The first time I heard that statement, I paused. I could not believe that someone would say that to me. Did they think girls with darker skin were not beautiful? I remember being in class and one of my male friends was talking about a girl he knew from a camp he attended. He told my classmates and me, "Yeah, she wouldn't be pretty if she was dark skin." Immediately I was taken aback. I asked him a series of questions in regards to his statement. I wanted to know how he could even say something so disrespectful when his own mother, grandmother, and baby sister were of darker complexion. I told him that he offended me and every "sista" of rich color. I saw this as an opportunity to educate him. **I informed him that complexion should not be the underlying factor of one's beauty, instead, it should be** what is in one's heart. **Complexion can indeed enhance one's beauty, not negate it. We, the world, should not belittle someone because of their skin. Yes, I agree that one can have preferences, but I do not agree with despising differences in our preferences.** Afterwards, he did apologize for what he said and hopefully he walked away with a better understanding of beauty. The entire conversation made me think of how some people in society can say subjective comments out of pure ignorance. **It is our job as young women to encourage one another to love each other in spite of our differences and to encourage our young men to do the same.**

12. TAKE CARE OF YOUR HAIR, PERIODT

"SHE GOT GOOD HAIR! HE GOT GOOD HAIR TOO!"

I feel like we have all heard this at some point in our lives. Now, what does "Good Hair" actually mean? Society has made many of us believe that "Good Hair" is only hair that is either curly, crinkly, wavy, soft, and/or long. Sometimes these "Good Hair qualities" are often associated exclusively to biracial individuals.

> **GOOD HAIR IS HEALTHY HAIR.**
> **IT DOES NOT MATTER WHAT ETHNICITY YOU ARE.**
> **IT DOES NOT MATTER HOW LONG OR SHORT YOUR HAIR IS.**
> **IF YOUR HAIR IS HEALTHY, YOU ARE GOOD. PERIODT.**

I have heard so many girls wish that their hair was curly or extremely soft because they think that would fit the definition of "GOOD HAIR" but at the same time, I have heard some girls with curly hair wish that their hair was more coarse and thick. I have learned that instead of finding beauty in what God gave us, sometimes we yearn for the satisfaction of society and strongly desire what we do not possess.

BE HAPPY WITH YOUR HAIR.
TAKE CARE OF YOUR HAIR.
LOVE YOUR HAIR.

I can remember one time I was getting ready for school. I decided to wear my powerful afro puff. My puff was a beast or so the eleven year old me thought, lol. I brushed my edges with gel, sprayed that leave-in-conditioner, tied my scarf around my head and felt like I was stuff. My confidence was on one hundred with my big, pink bow in my head. As I walked to my school bus eager to take on the day, I was not ready for the words my bus driver was about to say. "Darling! What in the world did you do to your head? It looks like you just woke up, got out of bed, and put a hair tie on it." Immediately, that eleven year old girl lost her confidence. I went home with tears in my eyes that evening. I thought all day about what she said and how her face was when she looked at my head. My mother was furious. She began to use words I will not put in this writing. My mother saw this as an opportunity to educate the bus driver on the *Beauty of the Brown Girl*. She passionately grabbed magazines off of our bookshelf and began to cut out pictures of women of color and their various hairstyles. Women with braids, dreads, weaves, afros, twists, straight hair, curly hair, and short hair were all cut out and pasted on a large sheet of paper. In a letter, my mom explained to the bus driver that every young lady has the right to wear her hair whatever way she desires and that it is important to show respect. My mom wanted to show the bus driver different women of color and hairstyles worn so she would not be alarmed throughout her life and to ensure that she would not make that comment again. A copy of the letter was sent to my principal, transportation supervisor, and superintendent. Ladies, if you do not have anything nice to say, do not say anything at all. I appreciate my mother for having my back during that emotional time. She encouraged me to hold my head up even higher and love my puff, with all of its fuzz.

BE HAPPY WITH YOUR HAIR.
TAKE CARE OF YOUR HAIR.
LOVE YOUR HAIR.
PERIODT.

13. DON'T LET YOUR SHAPE DETERMINE YOUR MENTAL SPACE

I am going to say it one more time….

DON'T LET YOUR SHAPE DETERMINE YOUR MENTAL SPACE. Y'all feel what I'm saying? Throughout middle school, my friend Janelle always compared her body to other girls and their bodies. Janelle thought that her hips were too thick and desired them to be smaller. She also thought that her breasts were too big. Many of Janelle's friends were very skinny so Janelle thought that she should be skinny like her friends. My other friend Nia was very skinny. Nia desired to have wider hips and bigger breasts. Nia thought that her slim waist and slender legs were abnormal. I have experienced insecurities as well. Often times, I have questioned my appearance as to whether or not I was too toned for a girl and people compared that to masculinity. It is important to talk about how you feel to someone you trust. Do not just keep it all bottled in because sooner or later, you will begin to allow the insecurities to make you feel worthless. For me, I was able to talk to my parents. They listened to understand, not to respond. They encouraged me through their actions and words. **They told me to walk like I was beautiful, with my head up high, and my puffs to the sky! They told me to think like I was a genius and encouraged me to read and act like a sponge, soaking up everything I could learn to better myself and lead others to do the same. They told me to talk like I was Miss. President, with confidence, compassion, generosity, and love. They told me that I was born a leader. They told me to love me, especially my body. I say all of this to say, LADIES, regardless of the size of your breasts, the width of your hips, or the shape of your lips, you must love your body and all of its dips. You do not have to have a slim waist and a big butt to be beautiful. You can be beautiful by being you and loving you.**

Our bodies are our bodies. It is very important that we take care of our bodies. Think about how much you take care of your cell phone. The cell phone is always charged and constantly updated. You just don't let anybody hold on to it, and you try your best not to crack it. **Whether you want to believe it or not, your body is far more important than your cell phone and should be treated with the utmost care, dignity, love, and respect. It is okay to work out to become healthier, but at the same time, when you look in front of the mirror, you should find peace when viewing from head to feet.** Self health and self love go hand in hand. Don't let your **SHAPE** determine your mental **SPACE**.

14. _

There is no specific amount of rules to help you gain self love. The line above is for you to write the next step! Loving YOURSELF allows you to take pride in who you truly are and SHINE!! **For every girl that has read this entire book, I ask that you encourage, uplift, and embrace at least one girl that you know**. Encourage others that their dreams will become realities, uplift them when times get rough, and embrace what makes them who they are. **We girls need to unite and empower each other. We are all beautiful. We all matter.** Imagine if every person who betrayed, bullied, and belittled me would have uplifted me instead. What if I let the naysayers, haters, and doubters get to me everyday of my life? You probably would not have been reading my book right now, you might be reading my obituary. **My beautifully and wonderfully made fellow young women of excellence, there is absolutely nothing wrong with you. You are not the problem; you are the solution. You are not a mistake made by God; you are his masterpiece. You are a precious jewel. You have to believe that. You have to have**

SELF LOVE ....
L O V E S E L F.....

"Follow me on Instagram @byrd_girl"

"Follow my book on Instagram @selfloveselfbook"

About the Author

Brécha (Bray-sha) Janae Byrd, author of *Self Love...L O V E S E L F*, is from a small town called Surry County, Virginia. As a child, Brécha loved writing. She wrote poems and songs on a consistent basis. Both of Brécha's parents are educators and at a young age, they knew Brécha had a gift in regards to writing. She started writing *Self Love...L O V E S E L F* at age 16 and finished after she turned 17. Brécha has one younger brother named Breyden and they are very close. Brécha loves writing, playing basketball, singing, and eating bread (pancakes, french toast, cinnamon rolls, etc). She is well known in Surry County due to her great acts of kindness, volunteerism, and support to not only her peers but the entire county. At her high school, Brécha started a club known as the SCHS Hype Squad, created to promote school spirit and pride throughout the county. Brécha knows that her purpose here on earth is to live to inspire.

"My name is Brécha. You don't hear that everyday. I was born to make a difference. I am that difference. I live to inspire."

Printed in the United States
By Bookmasters